Graham Handley MA PhD

Brodie's Notes on Oscar Wilde's

The Importance of Being Earnest

Pan Books London and Sydney

First published 1978 by Pan Books Ltd
Cavaye Place, London SW10 9PG
6   7   8   9
© Graham Handley 1978
ISBN 0 330 50135 6
Filmset in Great Britain by
Northumberland Press Ltd, Gateshead, Tyne and Wear
Printed and bound by
Richard Clay (The Chaucer Press) Ltd, Bungay, Suffolk

Contents

Page references in these Notes are to the edition of the play
published by Heinemann Educational Books, but as references
are also given to particular Acts, the Notes may be used with
any edition of the play.

To the student

A close reading of the play is the student's primary task –
but it is well worth while seeing a performance if possible.
These notes will help to increase your understanding and
appreciation of the play, and to stimulate *your own* thinking
about it: *they are in no way intended as a substitute* for a
thorough knowledge of the play.

The author and his work

Oscar Fingall O'Flahertie Wills Wilde was born in Dublin in 1854, the son of a distinguished, though amorous, occulist. Wilde's Christian names hint at the flamboyance of the man to come. As a child he doted on his sister Isola, two years younger than himself and the family favourite. She died at the age of ten, and years later her brother was to mark her memory with a touching poem, 'Requiescat', in verses of sensitivity and simple regret:

> Tread lightly, she is near
> Under the snow,
> Speak gently, she can hear
> The daisies grow.

This is a far cry from the sophisticated writing, the wit and repartee, the paradox of the comedies and the intensely macabre and supernatural effects of *The Picture of Dorian Gray*; yet it shows a permanent facet of Wilde's nature, a certain childlike consciousness that lay buried beneath the image of the 'aesthete' he so consciously cultivated.

In 1871 Wilde went to Trinity College Dublin, and there he was greatly influenced by a young professor who introduced him to the study of Greek literature and culture generally, a study which was to fascinate Wilde for the rest of his life. In 1874 he won a gold medal for Greek at Trinity College, and, in the same year, a scholarship to Magdalen College, Oxford.

Wilde quickly established a reputation at Oxford for wit and conversation; and came under the influence first of Ruskin and then of Pater. The former was Slade Professor of Fine Art at Oxford, and had a wide and indeed increasing reputation as an authority on art, architecture and the

Renaissance in Italy. At the time of Wilde's arrival at Magdalen, Ruskin was giving a series of lectures, the first part of which was devoted to the Aesthetic school of art in Florence; Wilde became one of his pupils. Ruskin stressed among other things the pre-eminence of beauty and the dignity of labour; and these ideas greatly influenced Wilde at first.

Wilde soon came, however, to regard himself as a disciple of Walter Pater, who was a fellow of Brasenose College, and who believed in the study of pure beauty, exalting the cult of personal experience above all constraints. He wrote of 'the desire for beauty, the love of art for art's sake', the complete indulgence of physical sensation. Wilde, ever impressionable, succumbed, becoming an aesthete – one who cultivates the beautiful in nature and in art. This made him an object of perpetual interest to the cartoonist, particularly those in *Punch*, while the Gilbert and Sullivan operetta *Patience* burlesqued the cult, and Wilde in particular. The sub-title of this play was 'Bunthorne's Bride' (curiously, an anticipation in part of 'Bunbury' in *The Importance of Being Earnest*), and Bunthorne is described in the Dramatis Personae as a 'fleshly Poet'; and describes his just-completed poem as 'a wild, weird, fleshly thing; yet very tender, very yearning, very precious. It is called "Oh, Hollow! Hollow! Hollow!"'

Another influence on Wilde was Cardinal Newman, the founder-member of the Oxford Movement, which sought to raise the standard of the Church of England. Newman joined the Roman Catholic Church in the 1840s; he became one of the most influential writers and thinkers of his time, beloved alike for his sincerity and his humanity. Wilde too was of Protestant stock, two of his father's brothers being Church of England clergymen; but Wilde himself was always to feel strongly drawn towards Catholicism; just before his death he was strengthened by the last rites of the Catholic Church, into which he had been received on the previous day.

Wilde took a 'double-first', and in 1878 won the Newdigate

prize for his poem on Ravenna. He went on to London, intent on becoming a writer, but attracted considerable publicity by his dress – often a velvet coat, knee-breeches, black silk stockings, a silk shirt and a large green tie. By now he was living a little beyond his means, and, to make matters worse his first play, *Vera* (1881), was cancelled on the eve of production.

Wilde embarked on a lecture tour of America, returning in 1883 after achieving considerable success. He then wrote *The Duchess of Padua*, and in 1884 married Constance Lloyd. By the following year he was writing reviews for the *Pall Mall Gazette*, and in 1887 became the Editor of *The Woman's World*. He held this position for two years. In 1888 *The Happy Prince* and a number of fairy stories were published. The brilliant essays of *Intentions* appeared in 1891, and the same year saw the publication of *The Picture of Dorian Gray*, the remarkable novel based on Wilde's own feeling as he watched a sitter in a painter's studio: 'What a pity that such a glorious creature should ever grow old.' A second book of fairy tales, *The House of Pomegranates*, also appeared in 1891.

In February 1892 the first of the successful plays, *Lady Windermere's Fan*, began its London run; it was built on a combination of dramatic tension (a mother saving her daughter's reputation and losing her own in the process) and epigrammatic verve; Wilde was truly launched as a fashionable playwright. Meanwhile he wrote *Salome*, which was refused a licence, and by the summer of 1892 he was busy on *A Woman of No Importance*. This was an outstanding success, though some contemporary critics accused Wilde of merely stringing witticisms together. He was by then spending a good deal of time in Paris, and at that time published his poem, *The Sphinx*. In 1894 he wrote his last two plays, *An Ideal husband* and *The Importance of Being Earnest*.

By this time Wilde had formed a friendship that was to change the course of his life. He had met, and been attracted to, the Marquess of Queensberry's youngest son Lord Alfred Douglas. The father was of an unpredictable, overbearing and violent temperament; the son, who hated him, had distinct homosexual tendencies. Queensberry considered that his son was the victim of Wilde's corruption; but despite the uneasy tension of this time Wilde achieved yet another success with *An Ideal Husband*, in January 1895. As Shaw put it in a newspaper review, 'He plays with everything: with wit, with philosophy, with drama, with actors and audience, with the whole theatre.' During the previous September, Wilde had written *The Importance of Being Earnest*, which established him as a significant writer of comedy. It began its London run in February 1895, the producer George Alexander having asked Wilde to cut the play down from four acts to three, which he did.

Queensberry attempted to ruin the first night and failed, though four days later he left at Wilde's club a malicious card which publicly implied that Wilde was a 'somdomite' (Queensberry's spelling). Wilde unfortunately responded, and by so doing changed the course of his life. He charged Queensberry with criminal libel; he had no possible means of assessing the backlash to come. Wilde, society darling, author of three plays running in the West End at this time, whose aestheticism had been widely lampooned, whose wit, culture and independent way of life were soon to be seen as degradation, was brought down, his career wrecked, his life shortened. Queensberry brought counter charges; Wilde was arrested and tried (twice), found guilty of unnatural practices (the term masked by the legal jargon of a sub-section) and sentenced to two years' hard labour. The judge's summing-up went strongly against him, the language employed being hard to comprehend in these times when the emphasis is on 'consenting adults' in sexual relationships. The result for Wilde was ostracism, initially a kind of martyrdom, and then the writing of *De Profundis* and, following his release, *The Ballad of Reading Gaol*.

After his imprisonment Wilde spent some time in Berneval, a small village near Dieppe, then moved to Paris. These last years were further marred by a succession of events calculated to undermine his own resistance still further. His mother died in 1896, his wife in 1898, and though some friends remained loyal and visited him in France, he drank more and more heavily and was often unwell. In November 1900 he died, after terrible pain, of cerebral meningitis.

The Wilde who wrote the most sophisticated comedies, who became a dandy and an aesthete, the supposedly casual dropper of epigrams, was the same man who idolized his sister and who wrote perhaps some of the most compassionate lines of verse we have:

> And all men kill the thing they love,
> By all let this be heard,
> Some do it with a bitter look,
> Some with a flattering word,
> The Coward does it with a kiss
> The brave man with a sword.

Those who vilified Wilde, indignantly perpetrating a mode of intolerance that was in itself degrading, failed to twist the verdict of posterity. Wilde was a man of many talents: a great writer in the medium of comedy and a near-great writer in others. He wrote one different, outstandingly macabre novel, *Dorian Gray* (indebted here certainly to the French writers he loved); and he was a master of the ironic-comic story and the fairy tale, and was no mean critic. Although he could say that there were two turning points in his life – when his father sent him to Oxford and when he was sent to prison – his intimate personal record is to be found in *De Profundis*; it is surely one of the most moving self-acknow-legments of error in our language:

I summed up all systems in a phrase and all existence in an epigram ... I grew careless of the lives of others ... I took pleasure where it pleased me ... I ended in horrible disgrace ... There is only one thing for me now, absolute humility.

These are not broken phrases but the continuous sequence of suffering in a man reduced and yet ennobled by the expression of remorse and self-recognition. Sometimes in his life he touched gold, at others he tasted ashes; it is our knowledge and awareness of these extremes that causes us to respond so warmly to the works he has left.

Students should read at least two of the other comedies and, if possible, one or two of Wilde's reviews, or accounts of the American way of life. *The Portrait of Mr W.H.* contained in *Oscar Wilde: Works* (Collins) is also strongly recommended, conveying as it does so much of the real flavour of Wilde. Here Wilde deals with a critical mystery of identity that still defies solution today: that of the central recipient to whom Shakespeare's sonnets are written. In Wilde's story, the false painting of 'Willie Hughes' costs a life; but the underlying psychological obsession to discover the truth about the unknown is as valid and compelling for all time as it was to the percipient Wilde. We know that he intended to develop the version we have here, and it is not without irony that his own Mr W.H. ('Bosie', Lord Alfred Douglas) was at least partly responsible for Wilde's downfall. Wilde was forty-six years old when he died. He has survived his time which, in its narrow and retributive justice, failed to survive *him*. It was said of Dr Johnson that he talked great literature and all England listened; it might be as truthfully said of Wilde that he wrote great wit and posterity has not grown tired of enjoying it.

Recommended reading

A Life of Oscar Wilde, Pearson (Macdonald)
De Profundis, Wilde (*Penguin*)
The Picture of Dorian Gray, Wilde (Penguin)
Lord Arthur Savile's Crime, Wilde (Penguin)
The Ballad of Reading Gaol, Wilde (Collins)

The four-act version of
The Importance of Being Earnest

The original manuscript submitted to George Alexander, as we noted earlier, was in the form of a four-act play. That version was drastically revised by Wilde in the light of the producer's comments, but it yields information about Wilde's methods of work, his sure artistic sense when it was put to the test; and it also shows that the printed versions of the play today lack some of the original 'witticisms', which had to be omitted in the cause of prescribed length. The interested student, knowing of them, may also be made aware of Wilde's tightening of his own structure when it became clear that cuts would have to be made. What follows here, therefore, gives some indication of the extent of the original and of the revisions that reduced it; and it also provides a kind of sub-text to the one we have, thus helping today's readers to a somewhat fuller appreciation of the play.

The first point of interest is that the opening scene in the original and revised versions – between Algernon and Lane – is virtually the same, conveying excellently the differences and similarities in attitude between master and man, the whole imbued with satirical intention economically conveyed. In the first version there are some additions to the dialogue between Algernon and Jack (for example, Jack declares that he doesn't know anyone called Cecily 'as far as I can remember') a deliberate cushioning of the lies he is going to tell. There are other instances in the four-act version of the plot that contain further background embellishment. For example, the original dining venue for Jack and Algernon was the Savoy, not the Willis's of the cut version; and this is linked with Jack's debts to the Savoy (more than £700) which later play a considerable part in the plot. Jack adds here, 'They are always getting judgements and things against me. They bother my life out.' The reason for this being cut is, I think, sufficiently clear – the statement lacks the neat twist or balance common in Wilde's best dialogue, and is purely there as an adhesive of plot that can later be dispensed with. It slows down the exchanges here, though it is interesting to note that Jack says he gets 'writted about once a week'.

Again there is a cut of a few lines that include the word 'inquisitorial' when Gwendolen speaks of the investigations of her fearsome mother: Lady Bracknell's original interrogation of Jack demanded to know if he had sympathy of any kind with the Radical party. Jack's reply (which was omitted from the condensed version) is a superb example of Wildean wit apparently lost to us – 'I don't want to put the asses against the classes' – yet even here the reason for the cut becomes obvious to the close reader. The next few lines in both versions have a witty interchange on Jack having 'lost' both his parents, thus leading to Lady Bracknell's tirade 'To lose one parent may be regarded as a misfortune ... to lose both seems like carelessness' – and a preceding laugh might inhibit the effect of this.

Thus the final version ensures that no political line can detract from the splendid dowager-caricature focus on Lady Bracknell. The latter's exit immediately after she has soundly berated Jack, underlining the fact that Gwendolen could not be expected 'to form an alliance with a parcel' likewise has cuts such as 'Kindly open the door for me, sir', almost as if the playwright realized that he might be overplaying his hand if he gave Lady Bracknell too much to say.

Further sections cut include one on fathers and mothers, but the first version contains witticisms worthy of preservation, for instance, 'Relations never lend one any money, and won't give one credit, not even for genius.' Later there is the odd-seeming change of 'influenza' to 'severe chill' when the 'killing off' of 'Ernest' is spoken of. Also omitted is a brilliant little dissertation on 'Life is a question of tact.' Act 2's opening, unlike that of the first act, is not the same; in the original, Moulton, the gardener, plays some part in the initial exchanges. The caricature element in his speech is recognizable reason for its being omitted later ('I don't hold with them furrin' tongues'), and later literary references to Schiller and *William Tell* are taken out of Cecily's German studies. Here too some pedantic utterances by Dr Chasuble on Capital, Labour and Socialism disappear, while Cecily's inward debate as to whether or not she should entertain 'Mr Ernest Worthing' is shortened in the interests of dramatic tension. A plot extension involving the sending of telegrams, which Cecily makes a point of knowing by heart since they are confidential, is not present in the three-act version, and this is important since it makes Algernon's declaration that Cecily is 'the prettiest girl I ever saw' all the more effective.

Chasuble suffers heavily from the revisions, often at the expense of a rather mordaunt facet of Wilde's humour ('Death is the inheritance of us all ... Life were incomplete without it'), and one can only feel that here perhaps Wilde is trying to maintain a consonant lightness of tone by such omissions. Chasuble also loses the fine 'In every child there is the making of a saint' when discussing the rash of christenings; and after that the dubious 'I am not by any means a bigoted Paedobaptist' goes too.

But the most interesting inclusion in the original is the introduction of one Gribsby, of Gribsby and Parker, Solicitors, who arrives midway through Act 2, armed with a writ for debt (from the Savoy Hotel, of course) for 'Ernest'; he is introduced to Algernon, the 'Ernest' of this scene. In the ensuing exciting exchange Algernon is threatened with arrest and also with Holloway gaol. Cecily (who has fallen in love with him as 'Ernest') is prepared to pay his debt for him, thus securing his release. Here Jack is faced with a decision, and agrees to pay the bill and thus free 'Ernest' if Cecily will promise not to speak to him ('Ernest') unless spoken to. Perhaps this is a needless complexity; at any rate it was dispensed with, though its entertainment value is considerable. Moreover, it enabled Wilde to cast one or two satiric shafts at solicitors ('As a rule they sit in stuffy offices all day long, neglecting their business'); and the scene involving Gribsby is full of verve, sparkling exchanges covering the further extremes of duplicity on which the plot is based.

Much of the dialogue, witty and pointed, is omitted in the early part of Act 3, and the loss to the final version is considerable. Miss Prism, for example, refers to the fact that 'Profligacy is apt to dull the senses'; and when Algernon declares his love for Cecily, the latter makes him repeat it so that she can record it accurately and fully in her diary. The arrival of Gwendolen, with the ensuing dialogue, contains few omissions – hardly surprising in view of the sugary duplicity of the conversation, every phrase of which is a stress-mark of hypocrisy. The 'charming room' of the original gives way to the garden in the later version, thus enhancing the irony and wit of Gwendolen's 'country' references. Towards the end of this act there is some delightful epigrammatic dialogue, which has unfortunately been lost in the excisions; for example, 'One should always do what a woman doesn't expect, just as one should always say what she doesn't understand.' And, 'It is much cleverer to talk nonsense than to listen to it.'

Act 4 of the original version and Act 3 of the revised one open in the same way. But in the exchanges between Jack and Lady Bracknell, where he is withholding his consent to Cecily's marriage with Algernon, one speech is cut that contains a scathing attack on the imaginative impotence of contemporary novelists. There are further raids on the pedantic utterances of Chasuble, and a 'maternity' speech from Miss Prism when she is thought to be Jack's mother. The first version has Prism resigning after the revelations, then being proposed to by Chasuble, Lady Bracknell giving them her blessing in a speech that is omitted from the final version. Other revisions cut out a reference to *The Green Carnation*, which 'seems to be a book about the culture of exotics'. But the pace of the unravelling towards the end cannot be slowed, and both endings are virtually the same.

The overall effect of the cuts is difficult to assess finally, for there is both loss and gain. Gain is found in the crisp maintainance of dramatic tension; while the excision of some wit, quite up to the standard of what we have in the final version, can only be accounted a loss. There are also indications that Wilde's satire – political, cultural, society-mocking – ranged more widely; though certainly in the final version these concerns are well preserved.

The essence of *The Importance of Being Earnest* is pace: of dialogue and duplicity; of epigram and paradox; of wit and wisdom; and one sees that the revisions were largely undertaken with a concern for the preservation of that pace. Nevertheless, one is forced to recognize that between the lines of the final version there is the indelible mark of the original, and that the original would probably have received the same critical appraisal, and the audience's enjoyment of the play would have been as great.

Plot and structure

The plot is straightforward. Jack Worthing, called Ernest
and in love with Gwendolen Fairfax, has a mystery about his
birth, which he reveals when interrogated by Gwendolen's
mother Lady Bracknell; he was left in a hand-bag at
Victoria station as a baby, and brought up by his guardian,
Mr Thomas Cardew. Gwendolen has always known that she
will marry a man named Ernest, so Jack realizes that he must
be christened. Meanwhile his friend Algernon, posing as
Jack's brother Ernest, visits Jack's ward, Cecily Cardew, and
falls in love with her. She too confesses that she could only
fall in love with a man named Ernest, so Algernon finds
himself in the same dilemma as Jack.

Lady Bracknell, however, arrives at the Manor House in
pursuit of Gwendolen, recognizes Cecily's governess Miss
Prism as the woman who had disappeared some years previously with her sister's child. All is revealed, and Jack
turns out to be not only Lady Bracknell's nephew but also
to have been christened Ernest. The three couples – Ernest
and Gwendolen, Cecily and Algernon, Miss Prism and Dr
Chasuble – will thus live happily ever after. Lady Bracknell
ends not so much as presiding genius as complacent mother
and aunt with two financially and socially acceptable forth-
coming marriages to her credit.

Wilde's sense of structure is splendidly theatrical. Although
the language and its resonances arrest our attention and
compel our laughter, there is a rising curve of dramatic
tension throughout. Take, for example, Act 1: after the initial
dialogue we are intrigued by Jack's secret; the revelation of
the cigarette case and the lies that attempt to cover that
revelation; the idea of 'Bunburying'; and the arrival of the
dominating Lady Bracknell. Within the act there are ₂

number of 'scenes', not in the conventional sense of a change of décor or emphasis, but a series of shifts, which move towards the climax of Lady Bracknell's superb exit lines: 'You can hardly imagine that I and Lord Bracknell would dream of allowing our only daughter – a girl brought up with the utmost care – to marry into a cloak-room, and form an alliance with a parcel? Good morning, Mr Worthington!' (Act 1, p 19). Even here the tension is not allowed to drop, for Gwendolen returns and Algernon, true to good farce positioning, eavesdrops and discovers Jack's Hertfordshire address. Thus Algernon prepares to Bunbury, and the audience appreciates the delicious irony of the situation.

The construction of this first act means that the opening of the second act must pick up the tensions. Wilde cleverly introduces two caricatures – Miss Prism and Chasuble – to slow the pace, then accelerates the action by the arrival of Algernon as Ernest; his falling in love with Cecily is predictable, but at the back of our minds is the knowledge that Jack has threatened to kill off 'Ernest' as quickly as possible. Consequently the action moves swiftly to the confrontation of the two deceivers, with Cecily holding the balance precariously – but able to tell Algernon of her own fantasy before it gives place to reality in the form of Gwendolen's arrival.

Wilde's comedy has been called static, yet Act 2 is notable for the *speed* with which situation succeeds situation. Consider Gwendolen's arrival, and the shallow acceptance and love which each girl insincerely manifests for the other; this soon gives way to a reversal of judgement, an expression of dislike and then, in self-protection against the men who have 'deceived' them, an alliance that is as dubious and superficial as anything that has occurred before. Wilde is the *nonpareil* of timing and grouping; and the patterning of contrast and parallel, opposite and like, simulated love and momentary hate are all the cornerstones of his sense of form. Built into this is a contrast between town and country – sophistication and apparent innocence; between rhetoric (Lady Bracknell) and languor (Jack); between appearance and reality. All reveal Wilde's sense of structure to be as sophisticated as the society he is describing.

The rising curve is maintained in Act 3, for it is this act which is dependent on the revelations for its dramatic and comic effect. Here we have the mock-heroic concept of men being prepared to be christened; Lady Bracknell's second interrogation, this time with the infinitely satisfactory conclusion that Cecily is more than well provided for; and then the wholly understandable determination of Jack to withhold his consent until his own marriage to Gwendolen has been conceded. We are in polite society, but blackmail under any disguise is of the stuff of dramatic interest. The final revelation is, of course, Miss Prism's – though Lady Bracknell's identification of the baby who now stands before us ensures that her own contribution is not unimportant. Again Wilde's handling of detail within the structure is masterly – Jack's cry of 'Mother!' provides an almost farcical climax before the final denouement of the complicated plot.

It is obvious why George Alexander wanted the fourth act of the play omitted. The structure here is tight, and all promotes the main action, giving the play pace and unity. There is a temptation to see *The Importance of Being Earnest* as something of an allegory; with all the characters who have escaped reality compelled, at the last, to face it. But it is a happy facing, and the lightness of touch is maintained to the end.

The modes of comedy

The Importance of Being Earnest has been called 'a world of delightful make-believe'. Certainly the artificiality of Wilde's style mirrors that of the society in which he lived. His principal method – for which he is famous – is the epigrammatic reversal of accepted clichés; the emphasis is on a graceful turn of language, and elements of farce arise as a result.

Wilde was a contemporary of the early George Bernard Shaw, and the 1890s saw the first performances of *Widowers' Houses* (1892), *Arms and the Man* (1894) and *Candida* (1895). Although none of these was initially a popular success, they indicated the nature of Shaw's range and his capacity to benefit from the talents of Henry Arthur Jones, Sir Arthur Pinero and Wilde himself, all of whom had been successful before him.

The major influence on Wilde, however, is not that of his contemporaries but rather the inheritance of Restoration comedy. The word-play, puns and affectations, the epigrams, innuendos and, in part, the farce of situation, are all present in Wilde as they are in Wycherley and Congreve, and later Sheridan. The differences are, of course, just as distinct. The notorious china scene of *The Country Wife* has no equivalent in Wilde, for his subject is not the licentiousness of his own times, rather their indolence and vacuousness. Wilde is not coarse, he is infinitely refined; his innuendos are decorous, without the tang of sexuality so manifest in Wycherley. Gwendolen and Cecily are not recognizable as descendants of Millamant or Mrs Fainall, nor are Ernest and Algernon comparable to Mirabell in *The Way of the World*, or to Horner in *The Country Wife*.

The late Victorian period is hardly comparable with the Restoration period, and changes in dramatic and literary taste inevitably reflect changes in morality. 'Aesthetic' and 'decadent' may be words applied to Wilde but half a century of repression had resulted in the society he pictured having its own areas of corruption. The nature of the comedy – verbal wit, deception and the image of a society watching itself being re-created on stage – Wilde has in common with Congreve and the other writers of comedy two hundred years before his own time. As George Rowell notes in *The Victorian Theatre: A Survey* (1956), Wilde uses stereotyped plots. For example, in each of the three plays that precede *The Importance of Being Earnest* there is a woman with a past; but in the final play Wilde shows himself 'a joyous rebel'. This is because *The Importance of Being Earnest* is itself a parody of the routines of comedy.

The lasting fact for us is that Wilde ridiculed both himself and his contemporaries, while Shaw picked his way through social and intellectual drama. Simply, Wilde confronts an essentially civilized and superficial society with its own attitudes, false values and indeed corruptions, establishing a comedy of manners that was to pave the way for Noël Coward in the twentieth century. In a sense the plays are not so much about people as about words. The characters live through their speech, which does not convey an integrated psychology, but rather the role, or the mockery of the role, they are playing. For Wilde the word's the thing, and the effects achieved often exist independently of the characters. What they do reflect are the superficial responses of a society which, considering itself by birth and inheritance superior, imagines itself to be 'on show' – conscious at once of status and of what is expected of a social élite. No ripple of political unrest disturbs the current of their verbal exchanges, and even the servants, in imitation of their masters' demeanour, exist in this rarefied world of indolence.

It would, however, be a mistake to believe that Wilde is concerned with realism or with reality; he takes good care to omit from *The Importance of Being Earnest* anything that smacks of the crude or coarse, though one suspects that he is inwardly laughing at his characters' cloistered existence – one which he had himself enjoyed at the expense of hiding his other life until private tragedy overtook him. He invented or adapted a scintillating, if artificial, mode of speech, and we are told that he frequently made a note of witticisms spoken by himself or others, so that he could incorporate them, suitably polished, into his plays. In *The Importance of Being Earnest* it is true to say that the 'verbal fireworks' contribute most to the nature of the comedy. The textual notes sufficiently indicate the nature of Wilde's humour and its range; here we need only distinguish between the various facets of it. The title is a pun, and punning runs throughout the length of the play. Wilde's customary technique is that of reversing what society would regard as the normal in proverbial or conventional speech, as, for example, in 'Divorces are made in heaven', or 'The amount of women in London who flirt with their own husbands is perfectly scandalous. It looks bad.'

Irony, too, runs through the play, and this is reinforced by a satirical tone, which castigates society by exposing it in action. Wilde's satirical intent with regard to Lady Bracknell, who calculates eligibility in a young man, joins forces with her own kind to form an implacable committee of acceptability, consigns her husband to an inferior position and browbeats all with whom she comes into contact. Through her, Wilde attacks the society matriarch who rules by verbal power and unscrupulous manoeuvres. The play is thus anti-feminist and anti-romantic, in tone as well as intent; with both heroines revealed as ruthless in terms of their possessiveness and their craving for sensation. Through them Wilde is attacking forms of education and non-education, as well as that conditioning for society of which Lady Bracknell is so proud. Wilde also aims a number of satirical shafts at snobbery – particularly the snobbery of birth – and at sentiment, pedantic language, melodramatic situations, and hence at his contemporaries who make use of them.

Perhaps the most salient features of his style are its balance, its joy in words and its economy. Epigram and antithesis are released at will for the audience's delectation. The wit is underpinned with all the nonsense and extravagance a lively intellect can devise. Remember Cecily's 'love affair' with Uncle Jack's wicked brother 'Ernest'; it is farcical yet at the same time discloses a day-dream world with which we can all in our different ways identify. To Cecily it is her reality. But it does not end there; for Algernon enters into the spirit of her make-believe, asking what he had done to have his engagement broken. The satire is evident, but beneath it there is a poignancy. If Wilde exposes sentiment and romance he also exposes triviality, for the whole play is built round a trivial preference – for a Christian name that carries punning moral overtones. By stretching to the farcical a quirk of human nature – the predilection for a name – Wilde underlines the affected morality characteristic of the society he describes. The double identity and mistaken identity themes (*Twelfth Night* gives a rather different treatment) are certainly central to Wilde's conception, here linked to the day-dream world of Cecily. But it is, after all, a man's world; so Jack and Algy can 'live' Ernest and Bunbury without having to resort to the substitute of a diary.

The concept is again farcical, but the escapist idea behind it is part of human nature; the part that seeks to make the dull present liveable by indulging in an imaginary, more attractive, life. So this section ends with words: with paradox, epigram, pun, euphemism and with a wit that is sometimes wisdom; all these embroider situations that are the staple diet of melodrama and society comedy. Add, finally, Wilde's parody of himself and of others, and you have the main facets of his art.

The characters

The characters in *The Importance of Being Earnest* are important for what they say and sometimes for what they represent; it cannot be said that they are psychologically significant, or even psychologically developed. They are largely one-dimensional, and their reactions are often conditioned by Wilde's opportunism, always verbal and exploiting the promise of a situation. One character – or caricature – dominates both audience and players.

Lady Bracknell

Until yesterday I had no idea that there
were any families or persons whose origin
was a Terminus.

Lady Bracknell represents birth and status, the rule of the matriarch in society. A shrewd business woman (though she would recoil at the term), her aims are to keep her husband in subjection, to marry off her daughter advantageously and to ensure that she maintains her position in society by being seen at the right houses. Always in good voice, she has a mastery of rhetoric and authority; only once is this undermined – when Jack refuses his consent to the marriage of Cecily and Algernon. Fortunately circumstances, in the form of the reappearance of Miss Prism, give her the opportunity of making the final revelation about Jack. Wilde has made a clever choice of name for her – Augusta – for she is awe-inspiring in her capacity for taking complete control; though there is a delightful moment of action in the first act when Gwendolen and Jack blow kisses to one another behind her back as she is about to go down with Gwendolen to her carriage. She has cast aside femininity (if, indeed, she ever had any) and substituted power, turning the domestic province of women into an empire of her own making.

Lady Bracknell is critical of those with whom she mixes, holds up Mary Farquhar as a domestic model to Algernon, and is very conscious of the proprieties, such as having the right number of guests to balance her own table. She lives by a particular creed – 'Health is the primary duty of life' – to which she insists that Lord Bracknell subscribes. She has the wholly unjustified English prejudice against the French, expressing her disapproval in terms of music. She has an acute sense of physical propriety among her own class: 'Rise, sir, from this semi-recumbent posture. It is most indecorous.' She believes that engagements are made by parents, and not by children. She unashamedly confesses to collaborating with the Duchess of Bolton, accepts ignorance as a 'delicate exotic fruit', and considers that education in England is irrelevant, being realistic enough to see that it has not changed the *status quo*.

She is practical and unscrupulous: she finds Jack's hand-bag origins unacceptable but advises him to acquire some relations. Absent for the whole of the second act, she returns to dominate the third. She has bribed Gwendolen's maid and come down to the Manor House herself; she undertakes another interrogation, this time of Jack concerning the status and birth of Cecily. She is won to an appreciation of Cecily's beauty after learning of her fortune; considers how best to improve her, in keeping with the demands of society; and gives sound advice on the undesirability of long engagements. She is only brought back from a direct confrontation with Jack by the entrance of Miss Prism. Lady Bracknell retrieves her own position by the revelation she has to make, though she accuses Jack of 'triviality' when he embraces Gwendolen. She is larger than life, with something of the Gorgon attributed to her by Jack.

Jack

It is very vulgar to talk like a dentist
when one isn't a dentist. It produces
a false impression.

Jack is in love with Gwendolen. His first remarks disclose
that he has travelled up to town for the purpose of proposing
to her. Like Algernon later, he eats by way of compensation;
is annoyed when he finds that Algy has his cigarette case;
and, though he is romantic about Gwendolen, is sufficiently
narrow-minded to wish to 'protect' his ward Cecily from
Algy. He is forced into admitting that he has two lives, one
in the town and one in the country. He realizes that
Gwendolen loves him for what he is not, and determines to be
christened. He is nervous of Lady Bracknell to begin with, but
stands up well to her cross-examination, even offering to
produce the hand-bag as evidence of his birth. After her exit
he says that he is sick to death of cleverness; adds that he will
kill off his brother Ernest; gives Gwendolen his Hertfordshire
address, and sees her out. Jack's next appearance is in
mourning; having convinced Dr Chasuble and Miss Prism
that his brother Ernest is indeed dead, he is horrified to
discover that Algy is impersonating Ernest, as a result of
which he is forced by Cecily to shake hands with him. He
does his utmost to get rid of Algy quickly, and is then
caught up in the mistaken identity with Gwendolen and
Cecily, an occasion which produces the painful necessity of
his having to speak the truth and admit that his name is
John.

Jack is appalled when Algy eats the muffins at the moment
of crisis, but when they next see the girls he is foremost in
asserting that both of them will be christened 'Ernest'. He
adopts a proud tone with Lady Bracknell at her second
interrogation, disliking her tone with regard to Cecily. He
detests Lady Bracknell's patronage and snobbery but has the

independence and cunning to withhold his consent to the marriage of Cecily and Algernon until his own future with Gwendolen is assured. But before that can happen he has to accept the revelation with regard to his own birth; after believing that Miss Prism is his mother, his place in society is guaranteed when he learns that he is Algy's brother and that Lady Bracknell is his Aunt Augusta too!

Algernon

I have invented an invaluable permanent
invalid called Bunbury, in order that I
may be able to go down into the country
whenever I choose.

Algernon is greatly expressive of his author's wit, and in addition is a much more experienced exponent of the escapist life than is Jack, for Algy has invented Bunbury as the refuge from the excessive demands of society – particularly those of Aunt Augusta. He is sharp, noting what the servants drink; is critical of Jack, eats as he pleases; and has discovered something about Jack that he intends to turn to good account. Having produced the cigarette case, he conducts his own interrogation, and then charmingly admits that he is himself a Bunburyist, a term he defines with commendable honesty. For some time Algernon has been trying to determine the whereabouts of Jack's ward Cecily, and he invites Jack to dine with him that evening so that he can avoid dining with Aunt Augusta. He is, however, anxious to ingratiate himself with his aunt, and goes through her music programme with her.

Afterwards, he overhears Jack giving Gwendolen his country address, notes it on his cuff, and arranges with his servant Lane to 'Bunbury' the next day. This he does, impersonating the wayward brother Ernest, and of course falls in love with Cecily. Faced with Jack's arrival, he keeps his head and promises to reform. He then learns of Cecily's fantasy about himself and their engagement, a fantasy he enters into wholeheartedly. He has to face the 'Ernest' dilemma when he learns of Cecily's love for that name. He arranges his christening, enjoys his exchanges with Jack – who is much discomforted at the turn of things – and proceeds to eat his way through the muffins. Algernon tends to be somewhat eclipsed in Act 3, since the dramatic development, while concerning him, more centrally concerns Jack.

Gwendolen

I intend to develop in many directions

Gwendolen is 'smart', both verbally and in appearance. She is self-opinionated, to the trivial extent that the name 'Ernest' is the centre of her existence. She is coquettish in a rather superior fashion and makes sure that she is proposed to at the most interruptible moment. Perhaps it is a small mark of independence of her mother. She vows eternal devotion, considers it necessary to have Jack's country address, and goes down to see him, encountering Cecily on her arrival. The result is a study in insincerity.

Initially put out by the fact that Cecily is young and pretty, Gwendolen responds to the news that Cecily is 'engaged' to Mr Ernest Worthing by examining her diary in order to prove that she has precedence. But the duplicity of the men, and the mistaken identity, drive her closer to Cecily in alliance against these men. Her own inconsistency and her (inherited) determination to dictate the course of events causes her to break the silence she has vowed to keep. She and Cecily learn of the sacrifices to be made on their account – both men are to be christened 'Ernest' – and Gwendolen's role in the final events of the play is best summed up in her own words: 'This suspense is terrible. I hope it will last.'

Cecily

I know perfectly well that I look quite plain
after my German lesson.

Cecily does not appear until Act 2. She is interested in
Jack's wicked brother Ernest, and keeps a diary in order to
record all the wonderful things in her life which, as she says,
she would otherwise forget. She is something of a match-
maker herself, suggesting that Dr Chasuble and Miss Prism
might take a walk together. She flirts with Algernon and,
when the moment is ripe, produces him to Jack and forces
the latter to shake hands with him. Cecily is complacently
happy after this, and deliberately contrives to be alone with
Algernon so that she can tell him of their engagement and
the manner of its ending, all the records having been entered
in her diary. Her exchanges with Gwendolen are sugary, then
unpleasant, and in the practical issue of putting the society
lady in her place Cecily manages to give her sugar and cake
– both of which Gwendolen has refused.

Like Gwendolen, however, Cecily responds to male duplicity by female alliance, albeit temporary; like Gwendolen,
too, she accepts the male movement towards christening as a
great sacrifice on their part: 'They have moments of physical
courage of which we women know absolutely nothing.'
Romance satisfied, Cecily is becomingly submissive to Lady
Bracknell. She has more colour than Gwendolen, mainly
because the diary revelations are a positive dream-life
compared with the elegant boredom that Gwendolen
endures.

Other Characters

Merriman is the conventional butler who acts on what he
hears and what he is told. *Land* is rather different. He
comments on marriage and the question of 'ready money'

in the market; both these areas are in fact themes in the play.

Miss Prism and *Dr Chasuble* are stock figures of farce; the older couple, redolent of propriety, who are used as a contrast with the romantic young lovers. At first, they exist in pedantic relationship to one another; then they play a part in the main unravelling of the plot. Chasuble is, so to speak, the focus of the christening. Miss Prism's role is altogether more important, since she holds the truth of Jack's birth without knowing it, until Lady Bracknell forces the revelation. From this we gather that she is inclined to be absent-minded, but her speech is full of euphemisms ('intellectual pleasures' for 'German grammar'). She affects to be puritanical (calling the chapter on 'The Fall of the Rupee' 'sensational'; Act 2, p. 29), though in reality she enjoys flirting with Chasuble. The latter enjoys using high-flown language on some occasions and academic allusiveness on others. The result is a stereotype who is ultimately able to claim the unscholarly Miss Prism – though we suspect that his has been a passionless celibacy.

Act 1, summary and textual notes

The time is the mid 1880s, the scene Algernon's fashionable room in Half Moon Street, Mayfair. Algernon is talking to his butler, Lane, about the coming visit of Lady Bracknell, and about marriage. Jack Worthing, known as Ernest, enters and begins to look forward to the visit of Lady Bracknell and Gwendolen Fairfax, to whom he is paying court. There is more light talk of marriage – and divorce – and Algernon reveals that he has a cigarette case belonging to Jack with an inscription which reads, 'From little Cecily with her fondest love to her dear Uncle Jack.' Much of the ensuing comedy centres round the double identity of Jack/Ernest, with Algernon himself admitting that he is a confirmed 'Bunburyist', meaning that he goes in for the same type of deception. ('Bunbury' is a fictitious relative Algernon is always pretending to visit, and 'Ernest' is Jack's fictitious wild brother, whom Cecily has never seen but merely heard about). Algernon does his utmost to discover the whereabouts of 'little Cecily', but Jack is devious, saying that he is going to kill off Ernest, since Cecily has become rather too interested in his existence. Thereupon Lady Bracknell and Gwendolen enter; and the older woman proceeds to dominate the conversation. Algernon, however, manages to avoid dining with her because of the illness of his friend Bunbury, who requires his attendance.

Lady Bracknell and Algernon repair to the music room, Gwendolen and Jack are left alone, and Gwendolen gives him her reason for loving him: 'my ideal has always been to love someone of the name of Ernest.' Naturally the dialogue which follows is rich in dramatic irony, Jack nearly revealing his real name, and pressing for an early marriage. Lady Bracknell returns to disturb Jack in his 'semi-recumbent posture' and follows this by a summary social check on his credentials. Discovering to her horror that he is an orphan, abandoned in a 'hand-bag' at Victoria station as a baby, Lady Bracknell firmly advises him to acquire some reputable relations. After she has swept out, Jack and Algernon discuss society, love, and, inevitably, Cecily. Gwendolen returns, Algernon eavesdrops and Jack gives Gwendolen his address in the country, which Algernon carefully notes down. While Jack sees Gwendolen to her carriage Algernon announces to Lane that he will be going 'Bunburying' the next day.

In this first act Wilde has been able to indulge to the full his satirical view of high society; the adhesive is wit, with a bubbling, adroit sureness of touch.

Pages 1–9

Half Moon Street Fashionable street in Mayfair, running between Curzon Street and Piccadilly.

I didn't think it polite The implication is that even the servants in high society do not what is natural but what is required of them; the irony suggests that culture is superficial rather than real.

Sentiment is my forte. I keep science for Life Note the balance, the precision of utterance, the inherent contrast (sentiment . . . science) and notice, too, that the contrast equates the emotions with culture, rational explanations with living.

the cucumber sandwiches This is in the era of afternoon teas. Here cucumber – largely water and somewhat tasteless – reflects the 'taste' of society, a further snippet of irony. The indolent characters in the play 'eat' rather than 'feel', or perhaps eat when they are feeling too much – witness Algernon's later demolition of the muffins (Act 2, p. 52).

I attribute it to the superior quality of the wine, sir Lane neatly turns Algernon's irony into the kind of snobbery his master represents, but goes on to indicate one of the penalties of marriage.

That was in consequence of a misunderstanding Wilde
frequently reverses the usual; here he is parodying the language
of the 'lower orders', who might be expected to refer to an
engagement as an 'understanding'.

I never think of it myself Lane's service life is more important
to him than his private life, and Wilde is attacking this reversal
of what is commonly accepted.

**They seem ... to have absolutely no sense of moral
responsibility** Here Algernon is reversing the accepted code
that the upper classes should set the pattern of morality for the
lower classes to follow.

**amuses oneself ... amuses other people ... excessively
boring** The comments, characteristically witty, underline the
indolence and vacuity of this way of life.

Why such reckless extravagance in one so young? Heavy
irony at the expense of Algernon, implying that he is conforming
to Lady Bracknell's standards of what to serve at teatime.

**I thought you had come up for pleasure ... I call that
business** One of the masterly features of the play is its
sustained satire, and Algernon's definition here of a proposal of
marriage exactly accords with Lady Bracknell's society practice;
to her marriage is a 'business' in which position, wealth and
birth have executive status.

The Divorce Court ... are so curiously constituted i.e.
people who 'forgot' about their marriages, behaved
irresponsibly.

Divorces are made in heaven The phrase is the opposite of
the largely romantic commonplace that marriages are made in
heaven.

Takes one and eats it Part of the comedy in this play lies in the
nature of Wilde's stage directions; eating forms the major area of
'action'.

She is my aunt The ridiculous nature of Algernon's self-
justification will be observed.

I don't give my consent This is the first time that the role of
the 'guardian' is mentioned. It is to be duplicated later with Jack
playing a heavy-handed role in relation to Algernon and Cecily.

I have been writing frantic letters to Scotland Yard about it This is Wilde's appraisal of high society's view that the police exist solely to serve its own trivial ends.

I was very nearly offering Again satirical, for who is to know what is missing unless the reward is offered?

now that I look at the inscription inside Wilde is parodying the use of this kind of device – the catching out or revelation – in more pretentious plays of the time.

half of modern culture depends on what one shouldn't read A reference to the Victorian habit of censoring the classics and Shakespeare, cutting out most sexual references.

modern culture ... in private Continuing the innuendo, implying that culture needs to be discussed widely – and probably is discussed too loudly and too often.

You have always told me it was Ernest The introduction of the pun central to the play's title and to the absurdity of its plot.

The Albany Exclusive apartments between Piccadilly and Regent Street (more correctly, simply 'Albany').

Bunburyist Algernon's equivalent to the different identities for town and country that Jack has described himself as having. The plot hinges on the ability to assume another identity, be mistaken, and to mislead others in the process. The word 'bunbury' is capable of ambiguous interpretation and association.

Miss Prism Again an almost Dickensian choice of name. In Dickens's time, and earlier, governesses set 'refined young ladies' to saying their 'prunes and prisms', an exercise intended to improve the shape of their lips! (Cf. *Little Dorrit*, Book 2, Chapter 5: 'Papa, potatoes, poultry, prunes and prism are all very good words for the lips; especially prunes and prism.') By giving the name of Prism to the governess Wilde is again stressing the artificiality of 'good society', as well as the affectations of the character herself.

into the most dreadful scrapes i.e. into trouble. Wilde frequently employs some fashionable slang as a further means of portraying the vacuousness of his characters.

modern literature a complete impossibility A satirical shaft at the improbabilities which constitute fiction.

forte i.e. strong point. See also note p.32.

who haven't been at a University Ironic aside at the lack of cuture displayed by those who write for the press – perhaps even a knock at Shaw.

Willis's A famous club founded in the eighteenth century but in Wilde's time a restaurant in St James's.

Mary Farquhar The choice of name reflects Wilde's own literary inheritance here; George Farquhar was a Restoration playwright (1678–1707).

washing one's clean linen in public Wilde has cunningly reversed the phrase (to wash one's dirty linen), thus emphasizing the fact that the standards of the society he is describing are the reverse of generally accepted ones.

Cecily is a little too much interested in him i.e. because of his wicked reputation.

you will be very glad to know Bunbury i.e. because he will provide you with a means of escape (from domestic tedium).

three is company and two is none Again a reversal of the accepted romantic notion and the catch-phrase that describes it.

the corrupt French Drama A reference to the fact that adultery, regarded as sinful on the English stage, is commonplace in French plays.

that Wagnerian manner i.e. heavy with foreboding, with tragedy. Again there is a play on words, for Richard Wagner's famous cycle of operas was called *The Ring of the Nibelungs*, and took the composer some twenty-five years to write. He lived from 1813 to 1883.

Pages 10–15

I intend to develop in many directions i.e. physically, mentally and emotionally, but the triple meaning is expressed, as becomes a well-bred young lady, without the slightest degree of coarseness.

she looks quite twenty years younger Yet another reversal, and a gibe at marriage, from which the lady has been fortunate enough to escape.

There were no cucumbers Lane immediately and automatically, lies to save his employer's 'face'.

Not even for ready money An oblique reference to the way so many of the rich live – accumulating tradesmen's bills.

turned quite gold from grief A witty reversal of the usual 'turned quite white'; an example of both the vanity of society women and the 'cattiness' of their friends.

one wants something that will encourage conversation Music here is merely a background for conversation, not something to be listened to.

French songs I cannot possibly allow ... But German sounds a thoroughly respectable language Lady Bracknell is voicing current prejudice: notice that she does not *know* anything about either language.

I knew I was destined to love you A mockery of the romantic notion of people being 'fated' to meet and fall in love.

metaphysical speculation i.e. philosophy of the mind, subtle abstract talk; here meaning not related to practical life.

It produces vibrations Gwendolen is perhaps delicately indicating a sexual response, but Wilde is also mocking spiritualism or psychic qualities in individuals. In the eighteen-nineties interest in spiritualism and mediums was considerable.

I must get christened Later Wilde is to explore fully the farcical possibilities of such a statement, and again the duality – with Algernon – is employed.

Goes on his knees This stage-direction is a deliberate underlining of the ridiculous, since it coincides virtually with the re-entrance of Lady Bracknell.

Pages 16–25

The same list as the dear Duchess of Bolton Note the emphasis on the *snobbery* and the fact that *eligibility* is the prelude to a *transaction* in Lady Bracknell's mind. Love, of course, does not enter into it. This is further underlined by, 'We work together in fact.'

in England, at any rate, education produces no effect whatsoever Lady Bracknell is, of course, referring to elementary education (after 1870). Her point is that if education had achieved anything the working classes would revolt.

Grosvenor Square is associated with the fashionable rich, and it has witnessed scenes of anarchist and political disturbance.

How many bedrooms The implication is that the best country houses must have sufficient bedrooms to entertain a number of socially desirable guests.

Belgrave Square The fashionable area between Sloane Street and Grosvenor Place.

the fashion, or the side Jack is being sarcastic and is put in his place by Lady Bracknell, who feels she has the power to effect physical as well as social change.

Liberal Unionist Those Liberals who, in 1886, quitted the Liberal ranks in order to join the Conservative (Tory) party in opposition to Gladstone's policy of home rule for Ireland.

Or come in the evening A subtle piece of snobbery: they are not *wholly* socially acceptable.

To lose one parent Notice that Lady Bracknell has already referred to these as 'minor matters', but this short speech should be studied again for its fine overturning of what is accepted (to be born in the purple means to be of noble blood, and here Lady Bracknell reverses the social standing of the aristocracy and those who make money).

a hand-bag A portmanteau, the equivalent of a grip today and therefore quite large.

the worst excesses of the French Revolution This began with the storming of the Bastille in 1789. Lady Bracknell, however, is not referring to the Reign of Terror but to the fact that people from humble beginnings rose to power.

acquire some relations ... before the season is quite over Again the unscrupulous nature of the remark is apparent, the 'season' being the time when everyone who is worth knowing is in town.

as right as a trivet The 'trivet' was originally an iron tripod for holding cooking vessels by the fire; 'right' means 'steady'. The phrase is proverbial and Jack here means that Gwendolen is reliable.

Gorgon ... a monster, without being a myth The one referred to here is Medusa who, in Greek legend, had the power of turning to stone anyone who looked at her. This is followed here by fine word-play, which stresses Lady Bracknell's monstrous presence.

I love hearing my relations abused Algernon is admitting to something which people generally conceal.

the smallest instinct about when to die i.e. so that they leave money to their (deserving relations) is what Algernon is saying.

apoplexy A rather unsuitable, hence funny, choice, since these attacks, which arrest the powers of sense and motion, tend to occur in people older than the supposed Ernest.

She has got a capital appetite Jack lists the unromantic qualities; the romantic ones would be the opposite: loss of appetite, limited exercise and long hours of study.

I lost at the age of three Expressive of the truth that parents grow away from their children once they have ceased to be children!

and marry often ... eternal devotion This speech, with its twists and turns, underlines the fact that Gwendolen is by no means 'as right as a trivet', but that she is simultaneously romantic, unromantic, calculating and wayward.

the *Railway Guide* The equivalent of the modern timetable.

to do something desperate Judging from what she says here, Gwendolen has in mind an urgent letter of entreaty or even elopement. It so happens that she merely visits Jack.

bills ... *tears them up* Again the emphasis on the fact that life – love – marriage – habit is 'commercial'. There is one law for society, another for the tradesmen!

that's nonsense ... Nobody ever does Good lines with which to end the Act – containing, as it does, an element of Wilde's self-mockery.

Act 2, summary and textual notes

Since there has been so much talk of Cecily, there is now a dramatic expectancy. We meet her straight away in the company of her governess, Miss Prism. Cecily is supposedly studying German, but her true interest lies in her own appearance. They discuss 'Uncle Jack', with Cecily writing in her diary from time to time. Clues are laid here, with Miss Prism remarking that she once wrote a novel herself. They are interrupted by Dr Chasuble; Cecily archly implies that Miss Prism has a headache and suggests that it would do her good to go for a walk with him.

Left to herself, Cecily finds that she has a visitor, 'Uncle Jack's' brother 'Ernest', who is, of course, Algernon. He is forced to assume the reputation which has been built up for him and Cecily urges him to set about reforming himself. Algernon's response is to make love to her in a flirtatious, flattering manner. When Dr Chasuble and Miss Prism re-enter, we find that their 'flirtation' (though they would never use such a word) has been proceeding along rather more academic lines, and we are immediately aware· of the contrasting effects that Wilde is producing.

Meanwhile Jack enters from '*the back of the garden*' and '*in the deepest mourning*' (p. 32). At this stage Cecily and 'Ernest' have moved on, so that Miss Prism and Dr Chasuble receive the news that 'Ernest' is dead – a fine comic device, which the audience is bound to appreciate, since 'Ernest' is at present talking to Cecily. Jack of course is only too well aware of the need to change his name, in view of Gwendolen's obsession with it, and arranges with Chasuble to be christened that evening. Cecily then appears, to announce the arrival of Jack's 'brother Ernest', followed by Algernon as 'Ernest', promising to reform in the future and apologizing for his wickedness in the past. Cecily persuades Jack to shake hands with 'Ernest' (who has been talking about his poor friend Bunbury!) and Jack and 'Ernest' are left together, Jack urging his 'brother's' immediate return to town.

Algernon, left to himself, ponders on his sudden love for Cecily. He prepares to take his leave of her, but his remarks are so impressive that Cecily insists on copying them into her diary – which, of course, she keeps with a view to later publication! The dog-cart that was to have taken 'Ernest' to the station is cancelled; Algernon confesses his love and learns in return that Cecily has been in love with the wicked 'Ernest' for three months prior to meeting him; Cecily's whole 'confession' represents a satirical burlesque of 'romance'. She now brings herself artlessly to the point where she has to confess that she has to marry someone called 'Ernest', so that Wilde is here duplicating the man's discomfort at his own duplicity and how to put it right. Algernon naturally argues for his own name (without revealing it), but he is treated as Jack was by Gwendolen when he spoke of his real name. Algernon, too, decides to be christened – a further under-lining of the plot's contrasts and parallels. Algernon goes off to arrange for the acquisition of his new name, and Merriman announces the arrival of Gwendolen to Cecily. There follows a sugary exchange between the two girls before Cecily reveals that she is 'Mr Worthing's ward', and this leads to the climax of revelation on each of their parts that they are engaged to 'Mr Ernest Worthing'. They then compare diary notes on the dates of their respective proposals. Christian names are dropped, and the acid of innuendo replaces the sugar of ignorance in their verbal exchanges. These insults are brought to a halt in front of Merriman, but Gwendolen is forced to accept the sugar and the cake which she had specifically declined.

Jack enters to disperse the misunderstanding, but is called 'Jack' by Cecily, thus confusing Gwendolen. Algernon, called

Ernest too, enters to claim his Cecily, though his name is revealed as Algernon. Both girls realize that they have been deceived and turn to each other in their indignation. They leave the men, who castigate one another; Algernon turns to eating muffins by way of relief. Each reveals that he has arranged to be christened Ernest at different times that evening; they continue to eat and talk.

Pages 26–32

utilitarian Useful, practical – here Miss Prism means 'menial'.

intellectual pleasures Miss Prism is nothing if not euphemistic; this is a high-flown way of describing the monotony of learning grammar!

he always lays stress on your German i.e. to keep you out of trouble, give you an occupation.

he often looks a little bored Cecily often makes little acidic observations that reflect the truth.

this modern mania for turning bad people into good people Undoubtedly Wilde had the Salvation Army in mind; from 1878 onwards it was very active in reclaiming souls.

As a man sows let him reap The original reference is Galatians 6, 7.

Memory ... three-volume novels that Mudie sends us Cecily is not, of course, talking of memory, but of fancy or imagination. Novels from the time of Scott's *Waverley* (1814) were frequently published in three volumes before being issued in a cheaper edition. Mudie's was a large circulating library to which people subscribed. They often took large numbers of the 'three-deckers', as they were known, thus ensuring that novelists like George Eliot, for example, reached a wide reading public.

I wrote one myself in earlier days A confession that plays an important part in the plot.

The good ended happily, and the bad unhappily. That is what Fiction means Another aphorism, true for the most part. In Victorian fiction it was a daring writer who led up to an unhappy ending, hence the controversy over *Tess of the D'Urbervilles* (1891).

Chasuble Again the name is important. The word defines the sleeveless vestment of a priest at Mass or the Eucharist.

my metaphor was drawn from bees Chasuble may be excused his confusion – he is thinking of 'Where the bee sucks there suck I' (*The Tempest*, Act V, Scene 1).

Egeria The nymph who inhabited a grotto near Rome; she was the wife and spiritual adviser of King Numa, hence Chasuble's meaning here.

Political Economy This was one of the new sciences in Wilde's time; and he is being satirical about its rise as a subject for study.

That would be hypocrisy A key phrase, though whether it can be applied to this level of comedy is doubtful. Certainly deception, lying and evasion are part of the froth of this play.

I have a business appointment ... to miss Again the reverse of what is considered acceptable – the keeping of appointments; yet another comment on the indolence of 'society'.

Your emigrating ... Australia A reference to the convention, in both life and fiction, that the 'black sheep' of the family was frequently sent to the colonies to begin life anew, make a fresh start, redeem himself.

the next world i.e. the after-life, a strong implication here of Hell.

to reform me ... your mission Again a reference to the Christian reformist zeal of the nineteen-eighties and 'nineties. Often society ladies were involved – Shaw's *Major Barbara*, for example.

Quixotic A reference to Don Quixote, the hero of the Cervantes episodic novel of that name, in which the hero is noted for his ridiculous (but lovable) knightly, chivalrous deeds.

A Maréchale Niel This rose has rich yellow flowers, and is of the noisette variety.

misanthrope ... womanthrope Only the first word exists, and Miss Prism has interpreted it in the narrowest possible sense, providing herself with an opportunity for verbal flirtation.

neologistic i.e. newly coined word or phrase.

the Primitive Church i.e. the Christian Church in its earliest times.

leads weaker vessels astray Note the cliché when Miss Prism has to deal with something delicate, like sex.

I spoke horticulturally My metaphor. This is tit-for-tat if we remember Chasuble's 'hanging on her lips . . . bees' remark earlier in the act (p. 28 in set book. See our note, p.42).

Pages 33–44

this garb of woe A deliberate parody of the high-flown speech expected of the 'stage' clergyman.

Charity i.e. show forgiveness.

the manna in the wilderness See particularly Exodus, 16, 14.

the Society for the Prevention of Discontent Wilde is obviously ridiculing the 'do-good' existence of such organizations (many still exist today) but again reversing the emphasis – 'lower orders' would usually be meant.

they don't seem to know what thrift is Miss Prism is implying with delicacy that the poor have too many children.

trot round i.e. come to you. Note the use of slang to undermine the spiritual associations of christening.

blessings in disguise The deliberate employment of a cliché to describe the supposed death.

resigned to his loss . . . peculiarly distressing Miss Prism is blunt enough to condemn what she regards as sinful, hence the idea of the wastrel brother's return is 'distressing'.

My little task of reconciliation Cecily is nothing if not smug.

the dog-cart Two-wheeled driving-cart with seats back to back.

a little over-dressed . . . immensely over-educated Again the antithetical balance, with a glance at public school and university education.

wildly, passionately A caricature of the language of the romantic hero.

Worn out by your entire ignorance of my existence And not, as would be the case in romantic courtship, by separation, trials and tribulations, parental objections and other sufferings.

I determined to end the matter The language of melodramatic romance.

He has never written a single book The implication is that too many people rush into print, on the one hand, and that others are too indolent to write anyway.

philanthropic work i.e. work on behalf of others. Cecily considers this 'forward' – one suspects because she has not the opportunity to take part.

I like you already more than I can say Here Wilde mocks the gushing insincerity with which people become attached to each other without reason, and certainly without knowledge.

such a comparatively short time A masterly understatement.

The home seems to me to be the proper sphere for the man A further reversal of what is usually accepted as 'a woman's place'. In the next few lines, Gwendolen exploits the paradox.

Pages 45–50

He grows more interesting hourly i.e. what is mysterious is attractive.

Modern, no less than Ancient History Gwendolen is showing off her education. Byron's *Don Juan* read of the loves of gods and goddesses; and instances of adultery in contemporary life would undoubtedly be what Wilde has in mind.

History would be quite unreadable Gwendolen, too, has her moments of self-honesty.

the *Morning Post* Then equivalent in status to *The Times*.

lorgnette A pair of eye-glasses usually held by a long handle.

It becomes a pleasure This speech confirms that Gwendolen has a good deal of her mother in her.

When I see a spade ... I have never seen a spade The delicate area of snobbery is being covered in this exchange between the two young ladies who have ceased to wear the 'shallow mask of manners'.

I had no idea there were any flowers in the country A further stressing of the ridiculous ignorance of high society, and the narrow enclosure of taste and fashion in which it lives.

agricultural depression Cecily is using the term commonly
applied to economic deprivation and suffering – a low standard
of living – to comment ironically on Gwendolen's affectation.

the aristocracy ... epidemic Again the physical diseases
usually suffered by the poor – cholera or diphtheria, for example –
are being cunningly used by Cecily in a metaphor to define the
disease of the rich; boredom.

Sugar is not fashionable Another instance of snobbery: note
that taste is the guide; whether or not sugar is beneficial is
immaterial.

My first impressions of people are invariably right A
delightful touch, indicating how superficial and hypocritical the
two girls have been in their immediate response when they first
met.

***The two girls move towards each other and put their
arms round each other's waists as if for protection*** A
fine stage direction, almost the beginning of a dance movement
which shows how conscious Wilde was of stage production. We
are almost into a mock-ballet, or comic-opera, when the joint
speeches start, with the sex-war epitomized by the girls sticking
together. The effect is pure farce.

Act 3, summary and textual notes

The two girls are together at the window, looking out on the garden. When the men enter, Gwendolen, having said that she will not be the first to speak, does so, but a comic technique is here used by Wilde to enhance the situation. This is to have Gwendolen and Cecily speak as a chorus, with Jack and Algernon replying in the same way. The reconciliation, negotiable in lieu of changed Christian names, is interrupted by the arrival of Lady Bracknell in pursuit of her recalcitrant daughter, and the dénouement begins.

In response to Lady Bracknell's questions Algernon reveals that Bunbury is dead. The interrogation is initially concerned with Cecily, but Lady Bracknell's tone of doubt changes when she learns that Cecily has £130,000 'in the Funds'; she inspects her with the practised eye of a society hostess, giving her blessing to her nephew Algernon, and her consent to the engagement. Jack, however, wields the real power. He refuses to consent to the marriage, since Cecily is his ward and he considers Algernon an unsuitable match. The ensuing battle with Lady Bracknell is hard fought. Jack lays down the conditions: he must be allowed to marry Gwendolen if Algernon is to marry Cecily. Lady Bracknell is about to sweep out with Gwendolen when Dr Chasuble enters; he mentions Miss Prism's name, causing a start of surprise in Lady Bracknell. Prism enters, to face the full force of Lady Bracknell's voice and interrogation. It transpires that Prism disappeared with a baby (and the manuscript of a three-volume novel) some twenty-eight years previously. She reveals that she deposited the baby in a hand-bag at Victoria station. Jack exits in great excitement, re-entering with the hand-bag so that Prism can identify it. The farcical moment when Jack calls Miss Prism 'mother' gives way to the revelation that he is really Algernon's brother, and that as the son of Lady Bracknell's sister, he has to call that formidable lady 'aunt'. Jack also learns that his father's name was Ernest, that he was himself christened Ernest. Miss Prism and Chasuble, as well as the young couples, are united and all ends happily.

Pages 55–62

Mr Worthing, I have something Notice that Gwendolen immediately does just what she says she will not do – speaks.

German scepticism Here a reference to Schopenhauer and other writers on philosophical doubt.

I nearly always speak at the same time as other people Not merely a comment, but true of a number of people.

beats time This stage direction strengthens the effect of farce.

moments of physical courage A reference to 'immersions', the 'sprinkling' which Chasuble said was involved in baptism.

University Extension Scheme Through its extra-mural departments, a University brings courses to members of the public who wish to attend them.

the Influence of a permament income on Thought Here Wilde is parodying the kind of elevated course title, and the abstract nature of university courses.

whose origin was a Terminus This, and parts of her earlier speech, show Lady Bracknell at her rhetorical and sarcastic best.

the Court Guides Directories containing the names of those who have been presented at Court.

I have known strange errors Lady Bracknell is hinting darkly at bribery and forgery.

in the Funds Government loans, always considered a safe investment.

I am not in favour of long engagements Her reasons for not so being are soundly put in the next sentence.

I suspect him of being untruthful A delightful underlining of the areas of deception practised in the play – and in society.

He is an Oxonian i.e. he attended the University of Oxford, a guarantee that he would tell the truth!

on an important question of romance The reversal again.
We would normally expect the word 'business'.

Pages 64–70

a passionate celibacy A fine example of paradox.

might expose us to comment on the platform Lady
Bracknell always has an audience of inferiors in her mind's eye.

Anabaptists They believe in re-baptism, or the rejection of
infant baptism.

remotely connected with education This is Lady Bracknell's
delicate method of stigmatizing the position of 'governess'.

In spite of what I hear of her Note that the humour lies in the
fact that all Lady Bracknell has heard testifies to the credit of
Miss Prism.

bassinette i.e. the hooded, wicker perambulator: usually spelt
'bassinet', and today usually means a wicker cradle.

and often convincing i.e. because they are violent enough to
win their point.

I hope it will last Gwendolen loves the idea of being part of a
human drama, as distinct from the society role she has to play.

Gower Street Running parallel to Tottenham Court Road from
Euston.

temperance beverage Miss Prism's description of a non-
alcoholic drink.

It has been a great inconvenience Triviality is the theme
here (why didn't she get another bag?); the memories of her dull
life, too, are trivial.

Yes ... mother Splendid farce, but Wilde is burlesquing the
melodramatic situation common on stage – the revelation of the
hitherto concealed past.

who has the right to cast a stone Jack appropriately uses the
kind of biblical cliché Miss Prism might be expected to use
herself. He follows this with two further clichés in support.

**Every luxury that money could buy, including
christening** The ridiculous nature of the remark is apparent,
but Lady Bracknell is in the full flood of rhetoric.

Army Lists The official lists of officers.

Cecily! At last! The one omission in this last scene is any word from Cecily. It may be argued that this would be superfluous, since Algernon cannot become 'Ernest', but it does mean that Wilde has not tied up all the ends.

Revision questions

1 Write an essay on the elements of *farce* that you find in *The Importance of Being Earnest.*

2 Estimate the importance of Lady Bracknell in the action of the play.

3 How far is *punning* important to our appreciation of *The Importance of Being Earnest?*

4 Discuss Wilde's use of paradox in the play.

5 Write a detailed appreciation of any *one* of the three acts, showing the theatrical skills Wilde displays.

6 Compare and contrast Algernon and Jack and say what each contributes to the action of the play.

7 How does the comedy of mistaken identity contribute to our appreciation of the humour of *The Importance of Being Earnest?*

8 In what way is the play an exposé of the society of the time? Refer closely to the text in your answer.

9 Write a considered appreciation of Wilde's use of epigram in the play.

10 Compare and contrast Gwendolen and Cecily, and indicate the role that each plays in the plot of the play.

11 How important is 'Bunburying' in the action of the play?

12 Discuss the use of fantasy or make-believe in *The Importance of Being Earnest.*

13 In what ways are Miss Prism and Dr Chasuble important to the plot of *The Importance of Being Earnest*?

14 Judging from this play, what aspects of his own society do you think Wilde particularly disliked? Give reasons for your answer.

15 Indicate the main elements of Wilde's satire in the play.

16 Write an essay on the importance of the stage directions in this play.

17 Do you think that Wilde had any serious intentions in writing *The Importance of Being Earnest*? Give reasons from the text to support your answer.

18 Which sequence in the action do you find the funniest, and why?

19 'Witty, but not good theatre.' How far would you agree or disagree with this judgement of the play?

20 'Strictly speaking, there is only one character.' How far would you agree with this statement?

21 Do you sympathize with any of the characters? If so, why? If not, why not?

22 In what ways do you think the action of the play is sacrificed to purely verbal effects?

23 'Completely lacking in action.' How far would you agree or disagree with this statement?

24 'Despite the verbal fireworks, it is dull and dated.' Consider this judgement in the light of your own reading of the play.

25 Write an essay on any of Wilde's techniques not mentioned in the above questions.

Pan study aids Titles published in the Brodie's Notes series

Peter Shaffer The Royal Hunt of the Sun

William Shakespeare Antony and Cleopatra As You Like It
Coriolanus Hamlet Henry IV (Part I) Henry IV (Part II)
Henry V Julius Caesar King Lear King Richard III
Love's Labour's Lost Macbeth Measure for Measure
The Merchant of Venice A Midsummer Night's Dream
Much Ado about Nothing Othello Richard II Romeo and Juliet
The Sonnets The Taming of the Shrew The Tempest
Twelfth Night The Winter's Tale

G. B. Shaw Androcles and the Lion Arms and the Man
Caesar and Cleopatra The Doctor's Dilemma Pygmalion Saint Joan

Richard Sheridan Plays of Sheridan: The Rivals; The Critic;
The School for Scandal

John Steinbeck The Grapes of Wrath Of Mice and Men & The
Pearl

Tom Stoppard Rosencrantz and Guildenstern are Dead

J. M. Synge The Playboy of the Western World

Jonathan Swift Gulliver's Travels

Alfred Tennyson Selected Poetry

William Thackeray Vanity Fair

Flora Thompson Lark Rise to Candleford

Dylan Thomas Under Milk Wood

Anthony Trollope Barchester Towers

Mark Twain Huckleberry Finn

Keith Waterhouse Billy Liar

Evelyn Waugh Decline and Fall Scoop

H. G. Wells The History of Mr Polly

John Webster The White Devil

Oscar Wilde The Importance of Being Earnest

Virginia Woolf To the Lighthouse

William Wordsworth The Prelude (Books 1, 2)

John Wyndham The Chrysalids

W. B. Yeats Selected Poetry

Australian titles

George Johnston My Brother Jack

Thomas Keneally The Chant of Jimmie Blacksmith

Ray Lawler Summer of the Seventeenth Doll

Henry Lawson The Bush Undertaker & Selected Short Stories

Ronald McKie The Mango Tree